HURRICANE HUGO

HURRICANE HUGO

FROM THE EYE OF A ROOFING CONTRACTOR

ED MURTON

Charleston, SC
www.PalmettoPublishing.com

Hurricane Hugo: From the Eye of a Roofing Contractor
Copyright © 2021 by Ed Murton

First Edition

ISBN: 978-1-63837-696-5

Contents

PREFACE

I started Murton Roofing of Miami in 1975. After waiting fourteen years for a hurricane to hit, one finally did—six hundred miles away. I went up to Charleston, South Carolina, to see if I could help. Murton Roofing was instrumental in helping the Charleston school board get the schools reopened. We did dry-ins for thirty-four schools and got them open and were awarded twenty-seven schools to reroof.

We worked with the South Carolina Ports Authority to reroof Building 318 and repair the administration building. Murton Roofing worked in the naval shipyard; we reroofed Building 198, which was the administration building, and Building 41. Murton Roofing helped several local people too. We did over $6 million in reroof work in Charleston.

Murton Roofing of South Carolina operated in three states: Georgia, South Carolina, and North Carolina. In 2010, I closed all three states and retired. I moved to Florida

My next book will be on Hurricane Andrew, which hit right in our own backyard. I have worked in ten major hurricanes from 1989 to 2005.

Key People

1. Terry Marshall—superintendent
2. Jerry "Bones" Doxie—foreman
3. John Bodine—all-around man, office
4. Sharon Robertson—office manager
5. Rich Murton—brother and partner
6. Ray Anderson—Charleston school board
7. Randy Walker—foreman
8. Esta Murton—wife
9. Stanley Waldman—lawyer and friend
10. Ernie Gore—Gore Industries owner
11. Nelson—foreman
12. Mary Wilson—owner of Rainbow Market

CHAPTER 1

Hurricane Hugo—Getting Up There

On September 20, 1989, I had just won the Calcutta of $8,000 in a Key West fishing tournament. My cut was $2,000. I chartered a plane from Key West to Columbia, South Carolina, and the airport in Charleston was closed. We arrived in Columbia at 11:30. When I arrived at the airport, I went to rent a car. It was the last one available. When I went to rent a room, they were all taken. I was told that Allstate insurance had rented all the rooms, so I lied and told the hotel clerk that I was an Allstate adjuster and got a room.

The next morning, I left the hotel and headed to Charleston to check out the damage that Hurricane Hugo had caused. When I got about ten miles out, there were roadblocks. I told the officer that I was a roofer and that I was looking for city hall or the building department. He said, "Follow me," and gave me an escort. When we got down to East Bay Drive, I found the building department was in a five-story brick building. When I got to the building department, I told them I was from Miami and that I needed a South Carolina license to do work in South Carolina. They said they would need my insurance and that it would take two to three weeks to get the license. They also told me that the building needed a roof and that the manager was in his office on the fifth floor. I walked up five flights of stairs.

The manager, Mr. Jackson, told me that he had wooden floors, and he was afraid if they got wet, they would buckle. He took me up to the roof. It was half gone, and the wooden deck was showing. Now I was only there to get a license to work in Charleston, so I did not have anything with me to measure the roof. Mr. Jackson told me he had the blueprints for the building in his office. After I looked around at the damage, we went back down to his office. The building used to be a cigar factory. I was given a little office to go over the blueprints and figure out a cost for the roof. That number ended up being $140,000.

I called my brother Rich down in Miami on my mobile phone and told him what was going on. He was a little hesitant, but our company, Murton

Roofing of Miami, was in trouble financially. We had a debt of $1 million with our suppliers. He agreed to the job but said that Mr. Jackson would have to give us a $50,000 deposit to get things rolling.

I met with Mr. Jackson in the morning and went over the cost of the job and the amount of the deposit needed to get the job rolling. I also told him that I was not licensed in South Carolina yet and that it would be a two- to three-week wait before I would have the license. He told me that he would take care of that, and then he asked me to wait while he made a phone call. It was about a five-minute wait, and then he came out of his office with a check for $50,000. He said, "We have a deal," and told me to get him the contract and start work. He went down to the building department and came back with my license. He said I could use the little office that I was working in. Within two days of being in Charleston, I had a contract for $140,000, my license, an office, and a check for $50,000.

I called Rich and told him what I needed. I needed Terry Marshall, who was our main foreman, and his right-hand man, Jerry Doxie, as well as two high-lift trucks with a kettle and a crew of six men. Rich said he was on it. I gave him a list of materials too. He called Peter Daniels, president of Presidential

Supplies, and asked him if he wanted to go up to Charleston, and he agreed. The next morning, the trucks left Miami and headed to Charleston. Now I had the job of finding a place for the crew to stay. The closest place I could find was in St. George on I-95, about fifty miles from Charleston. The hotel had roof damage, and I made a deal with the owner to make repairs on the roof in exchange for the rooms for my crew. That evening, the trucks arrived.

The next morning, the crew arrived on the job. They were setting up, and I was in my office. I was having trouble with my phone, so I went next door. There was a lady named Sharon Robertson there. I asked her if I could use her phone to make a call, and she said yes. While I was on the phone, her boss came into the room. He was upset and started yelling at her for allowing me to use the phone. I went back to my office, shaking at what happened. After her boss left, I went back over to tell Sharon that I was sorry for what happened. I asked her how much he was paying her; she said, "Eight dollars per hour."

I told her I would pay her fifteen dollars an hour, and she packed up all her stuff and moved over to my office. Sharon told me that she had two teenage daughters and that she was divorced. She also said she was a local girl and knew a lot of people in town.

The next morning, when she came into work, she said she knew a guy named Ray Anderson who worked for the school board, and he needed help. There were only three commercial roofing companies in town. I asked her to set up a meeting with Ray, and she said that would be no problem. She got ahold of Ray and set up the meeting for the morning.

The next morning, I met up with Ray. He was in charge of all the schools' reroofs. He gave me three schools to look at and asked for a price to dry them in. That afternoon, Terry and I went and looked at all three schools. That night, I figured out the price. In the morning, I met with Ray and gave him the price on all three schools. He asked if I needed a purchase order to get started. I left Ray's office with three purchase orders. I met with Terry that afternoon. He already had Mr. Jackson in the dry. He was so relieved. I told him I had to pull off for a couple of days, and he said he understood.

The next morning, we were on the first school. At the end of the day, we had it dried-in. On the second day, we dried in the other two schools. The next morning, I met with Ray. He was impressed. I told him I needed to get paid for the three POs. He said, "No problem," and went and got me a check. He gave me three more schools to look at. We were hooked up with the school board within six days, all thanks to Sharon. I had Sharon looking at warehouses for me. She said that she might have a place for me in North Charleston. She knew the owner, Stanley Waldman, and set up a meeting with him.

When I met with him, I learned he had a small building on Remount Road. It had a fenced-in yard. It was perfect, except that it did not have an office. There was a strip shopping center that had offices on the second floor next to the warehouse. Stanley owned that too. He told me he could rent me an office in there. I now had an office and a warehouse in North Charleston. We moved our little office into our new office. We had an address now. The new office was great for Sharon. She lived two minutes from it, and her daughters went to school right behind it.

The next three schools were the same as the previous. Ray gave me the POs for all three dry-ins. Terry made short order of all three. I had to order material. Peter sent up two trucks full of materials. We unloaded them into the new warehouse. While talking with Ray, I found out he had forty-eight schools that needed dry-ins. When the dry-ins were complete, he would come out for bids on new roofs.

CHAPTER 2

Charleston School Board

We finished Mr. Jackson's work and got paid for it. All in all, with the school board money, I sent $200,000 down to Miami by November 1. We were on our twelfth dry-in, and Ray was issuing more POs. We hired some local men from St. George. There was a trailer park right next to the warehouse, so I rented four trailers and moved the crew in. These guys could now walk to work.

One day, when I came to the warehouse, there was a truck with a kettle on it and a crew of five. There was also a car with the truck. Randy Walker was the owner of a roofing company from Panama City, Florida. He was looking for work. Ray gave me a job to look at. It was Memminger Auditorium. It was three stories and a difficult job. I gave Randy the address and told him to go look at it and give me a price to do it. He came back with the price. I put some money on it and met with Ray. He gave me to POs to do it. I told Randy he had it. It took him five days to do the job. I went and checked it out. It was good work. I had Randy to help me out, and I was working seven days a week.

Eastern Airlines had a direct flight to Miami. Terry, Jerry, and I had to go home for the weekend. Terry and I got a room at the Meeting Street Inn. It was nice. One night, we were drinking, and when we came home and entered the room, there was a family in it. We were drunk and started swearing, and then we found out we were on the wrong floor. The next morning, we were asked to leave, and now we did not have anywhere to go.

The next day, I met with Stanley. He was an attorney and had an office next to mine. I asked him if he knew anybody with a place for rent. He said, "I have an idea." He said he had two condos in Mount Pleasant. It was a new project. He gave me the address and told me to go look at them and see what I thought. Terry and I went to look at them. They were brand new and had just been completed. I went back and met with Stanley.

He said, "You gave me a price to reroof the strip center we were in. It was $128,000. You put a new roof on my center, and I will give you the two condos, I will transfer the titles into your name." He told me to think about it. I told him we had a deal. We moved in that day; it was perfect!

The next weekend, I had Randy and his crew, plus my crew. We had fourteen men on the roof Saturday and Sunday, and we finished it. Monday, Stanley had all the papers ready for the transfer of the condos. I put one in my name and the other one in Terry's name. We could not believe it: two brand-new condos. Terry and I both invited our wives to come up for Christmas so they could see for themselves.

Jerry Doxie and his wife, Mary, had a little baby. She flew up to visit Jerry. I made a deal with them: if they could find a house at a reasonable price, I would give them the down payment. I already knew we were going to be there for a couple of years. They found a house in North Carolina. I gave them the down payment, and they bought the house. Mary moved up, and to this day, they still live there. They have been there for over thirty years.

It was late November or early December, and the weather was bad. We were still working on dryins. I met with Ray's boss, Mr. Thames. He told me that he had hired a consulting company from North Carolina, Robert M. Stafford, and they were going to write all the specs for the new roofs. He wanted me to meet with them and help them in any way I could. I agreed. He told me they would be starting after the first of the year.

We were on our eighteenth or nineteenth temporary dry-in. I sent another $100,000 down to Miami; my brother Rich had gotten some good jobs, and we were almost out of the woods with the debt. I told them to get our bonding in order and that all these reroofs would require a payment and performance bond with the bid. Matson Bonding was our agent. I called Duffy Matson and told him to get ready. He said, "Bring it on."

Ray told me he had a big school out in McClellanville, South Carolina, that had a lot of damage. The name of the school was Lincoln High. It was about thirty miles away, but it was still in the Charleston County School District. He asked while I was out there, could I check on another school, Saint James? I drove out to Lincoln High. It had no roof at all. I told Ray it would be a major repair. He said he had to do something on it now. He couldn't wait for the new roof. He was under a lot of pressure. It was two weeks before Christmas. I told Ray it would be $40,000, and he said he had to go with it and that I could start the next day.

We dropped everything and started the next day. After two weeks and Christmas Eve, we finished. My wife was coming up for the holidays; she wanted to check out the beaches.

CHAPTER 3

Folly Beach

It was New Year's Day. I was driving down Highway 171. Folly Beach was closed to all traffic. It was just open. My wife said, "Let's go check out all the damage."

When we got to the end of the road, we were in Folly Beach. We turned right to go down to the state park. When we got down about halfway in front of 609 West Ashley, we saw a for-sale sign. It was oceanside. We stopped and got out to look at it. There were some bikers staying there, and the first floor was completely filled with sand. This house was in bad shape. Four out of five houses on the island had been destroyed. My wife decided to call the number on the for-sale sign. The agent answered the phone and told us that she had just had a baby and would not be in the office until January 3. My wife and I agreed that if the price was anything between $150,000 and $200,000, we would be interested. Then the agent told us the price was $79,000, and we could not believe it. We had been looking at houses in Florida that were over $300,000. We wanted this house. We wanted to live on the water. We made an appointment to meet with the realtor on January 3. When we met with the agent, we drew up a contract for the full asking price along with a $10,000 deposit and close in thirty days. I knew with 80 percent of roofs being damaged in Charleston that I would be there for three or four years. This was perfect for me and my wife, Esta. She could move up here to Charleston, and we could sell our house in Miami.

Esta flew back to Miami, and I met with Stanley the next day and asked him to handle the closing. He agreed. About ten days later, Stanley asked me to come to his office. He told me that the owner, Dr. Nichols, wanted to back out of the deal. He said his daughter and her husband had been living there and gave the bikers permission to stay there. The doctor got mad and listed the house for sale. I told Stanley to go ahead and set up the closing. In five days, he had all the papers for the closing.

When the day for closing came, Dr. Nichols showed up without a lawyer. He said he was prepared to give me my $10,000 back plus $10,000 more to get out of the deal. I refused, and the closing took place.

The first thing I did after closing was go to the house and talk to the bikers. They said they were looking for work. There were four of them there with their girlfriends. I told them I would hire them to shovel all the sand out of the first floor. There was a lot! They agreed. Everything was going well until an inspector came to the house and said he was going to condemn the house. I went down to city hall to talk with the mayor, Bob Linville. I told him there was no structural damage to the house. He said he would talk with the inspector and get back to me. When he finally got back to me, he said there was no electricity in the house. I called the electric company, and they told me I would have to put a new service in and disconnect and rewire the house before they could hook up.

With all my luck, there was a guy named John Bodine who was living at the state park in a tent. He was an electrician who was looking for work. I hired him and bought all the material needed for the job. Within a week, John had the new service in. I called the electric company and set up a meeting with them. They came out and hooked up my service. I let John and his girlfriend move in. The first floor was all clean, and the electric was turned on. When I went to talk to Bob Linville again, he told me that there was a new ordinance that all structures had to be built twelve feet off the ground. I told him that I had renters in the house and that the inspector could not condemn the house. He agreed. In the end, 609 West Ashley was one of eleven houses that were grandfathered in that could have a first floor on Folly Beach.

John Bodine was a good all-around man. I hired him and put him on my payroll. He was in charge of the remodeling of the house. It needed new windows, floors, drywall, and siding, along with a new roof and a new air-conditioning unit. John built a new deck around the house that went out to the water. It would take him six months before it was complete.

Folly Beach House

Folly Beach

CHAPTER 4

School Board Jobs

It was January, and we had about twenty-five schools open. In some cases, we just did dry-in in the cafeteria and kitchen. We left the classrooms undone. Ray was wanting us to go back and dry-in the classrooms. Randy Walker was working out well for us. He was going back and doing the dry-ins in the classrooms. Ray wanted us to go back and finish Saint James-Santee School.

Going into February and March, the weather was bad. It was hard to get anything done. By April, we had almost all the schools open. We had another meeting with Ray and Mr. Thames. Mr. Thames said they estimated about $10 million to $15 million for the new roofs, and they were coming out with three new roofs designed by Robert M. Stafford. They

invited five contractors to attend the prejob conference, three local contractors, one from Alabama, and
me. The one from Alabama was States Roofing and
Sheet Metal Co. They had been helping with the temporary dry-ins.

When the day came, all five contractors showed
up. The prebid conference was mandatory. The representative from Robert M. Stafford explained all
the details for each school. The bid was due in ten
days. The requirements were the same as for the jobs
I had been bidding in Miami. They required a bid
bond, along with a bid form. You had to acknowl-
edge any addenda to the specifications. This was
new to Sharon in the office. I had her make a check-
list of everything that was required. Sharon was
good on detail. We sent down to Miami for the bid
bond. Terry Marshall and I visited all three schools
and measured them.

When the ten days were up, the five contractors showed up for the opening of the bids. Murton
Roofing won two schools, and State Roofing won the
third school. The other three contractors had high
bids, but they had plenty of work. I had three crews
now. Jerry Doxie had a crew, and I had Randy Walker.
We had to have a meeting with the principal of each
school and got to work on both schools.

The next bid was for two more schools. The same contractors were invited, but only two of the locals showed up. Murton Roofing was the lowest bidder on both schools, and States Roofing and Sheet Metal of Alabama was second.

Mr. Thames asked me to stay after the bid opening. He asked me if I had enough crews to get all this work completed. I told him I could handle it, and if not, I would get crews from Miami. I had over $400,000 in contracts, and it was just the start of thirty-eight schools that needed reroofs. Over the summer, seventeen more schools came out. I won nine of them, and States Roofing of Alabama won the other eight. We were the only two companies that were bidding responsibly. I had to get a sheet metal crew. I hired a man from Folly Beach. His name was Dave. His wife was a member of his crew, and they did good sheet metal work.

I won the bid for Ladson Elm. When I went to start it, I met with Nelson and David. They said they could handle it, so I hired both of them. Now I had five crews and over $1 million in contracts.

My house in Folly Beach was complete, and my wife had sold our house in Miami. She moved up to Folly Beach. John Bodine was a good man for measuring roofs and putting the bids together with me.

I was surprised at how hot it was in Charleston in July. We had to start work at 5:30 a.m. and be done by 2:00 p.m. It worked out for the schools too. We would be working when the kids got there at 8:00 a.m. and be gone when they got out at 3:30 p.m.

In the fall, I won a school called River's Elementary. It was a slate reroof. I met this guy named Rich. He was from Vermont and had been doing slate since he was sixteen. He had his own crew. He had been watching this job and saw who won it. When he came to me, he said he was the best slater in the country and he knew where to get the slate that was specified. We ordered the slate from Vermont. It was a lot cheaper than we had estimated. Stafford put an inspector on the job full time. Rich did a fantastic job and made me a believer. He *was* one of the best.

Over the next year, we won twenty-seven schools and became one of the biggest roofing companies in Charleston. In all, we did over $4 million in school work.

CHAPTER 5

Gore Industries

Stanley asked me if I could help out one of his friends. His name was Ernie Gore, and he owned Gore Industries. Stanley gave Ernie a call and set up an appointment for the next day.

When I met Ernie, he was very concerned that I was from Miami. Ernie said that he was using a local roofing company called Pelham Roofing. They were the biggest local roofing company in Charleston. He had already spent $70,000 with them, and he had more leaks than before they started. Gore Industries was a big plant that manufactured showcases for department stores. The building was 150,000 square feet. Ernie wanted a price on a total reroof. He asked me what the best roof out there was, and I told him that would be a four-ply and gravel from the Koppers company. It was a coal-tar system with a twenty-five-year warranty, but it was very expensive. He told me to price it for a Koppers roof. There were some units on the roof that he wanted to replace with new ones.

When I got up on the roof, I saw it was a mess. The temporary patches were already coming open, and the building had about twenty-five leaks throughout.

I got John Bodine to look at the damaged units and price them. When I got down and met with Ernie, I told him that I would get back to him in about two days. He said he wanted five names and phone numbers of people I had worked with in Miami. I told him I would have Sharon get it together and send it to him.

I was working with a distributor out of Atlanta called Heely-Brown. I told them I wanted to price the pitch in bulk delivery. I had a pitch tanker that would hold three thousand gallons of pitch. It would take seven loads of pitch; this would equal 165 tons of pitch. Heely-Brown was not familiar with bulk orders. No one had a three-thousand-gallon tanker. I told them to get ahold of the Koppers representative in the Charleston area. It was the same representative as in Atlanta. They got all the prices together.

I had to price the river-rock gravel to meet the specifications. I was familiar with that requirement because Murton Roofing of Miami had been doing the Koppers specification on Dade County schools. John was getting the prices together for the units.

In the meantime, Ernie had been calling the references Sharon gave him. When I went to meet with Ernie, the price on the estimate was $1,482,000. This included the units and a twenty-five-year warranty. This was the biggest job I had to date with Hurricane Hugo. When we went over the price on the estimate, Ernie wanted a payment and performance bond. This would be difficult. I already had all the schools bonded. I told him I would get back to him the next day.

I called the bonding company. They were hesitant. They wanted to know what account Ernie had the money in. Miami was hesitant too; they wanted a 30 percent deposit. The bonding company agreed after talking to me, as long as they knew where the money was. When I met with Ernie the next day, I told him what the bonding company wanted. He said the money was under his pillow. When I told him that the deposit was $440,000, he laughed at me. He said he would give me a $100,000 deposit and would sign the contract for $1,400,000 after he got the bond. He said he would give me weekly draws on work completed. That was the deal, and I was to call him when I had the bond. I was not going to lose this deal when I had $500,000 in profit for it.

When I called the bonding company and told the agent what Ernie had said, he said, "I hope you know what you're doing." He sent the bond up. I met with Ernie with the bond in hand. He was true to his word; he signed the contract and gave me a check for $100,000 and told me to start as soon as I could. I called down to Rich and told him I had a contract for $1,400,000 and a check for the $100,000 deposit.

This job had Terry Marshall's name all over it. Terry had been doing schools in Miami with the same specifications—Koppers four-ply and river rock. He knew those specifications well.

The first thing we had to do was get the tanker up to South Carolina. The name of it was "Big Red." Rich got a company to bring it up. It made the trip to South Carolina with no problems. Next, we had to get propane hooked up. We made a deal with a local propane company and had to pay them weekly because we had no account. I called Heely-Brown and told them I was ready for my bulk load of pitch. They set it up. It was coming from Alabama. The order arrived in two days with twenty-four tons of pitch. The tanker was up and running. The materials arrived at the same time. It had been one week since Ernie signed the contract. Terry was working and had started in the worst area.

Ernie was impressed. After the second week, I gave Ernie a draw on the work completed. He had my check ready within an hour. I told John to order the units, and he said they would be ready in two weeks. I called Heely-Brown and told them to call the Koppers representative and tell them we were ready for an inspection. Rich said he was relieved that everything was going smoothly. I told Heely-Brown that I would need a load of pitch weekly. I was in a hurry to get this job 100 percent complete so I could get it off my bonding. Plus, the money was good.

In the fifth week, we were ready for the rock. I ordered it from North Carolina. I needed fifteen truckloads. I had to rent a conveyor, and Terry started to rock in. It took five days. The job was 100 percent complete, including the units.

When I gave Ernie the final bill, he said he was going to hold 10 percent until he got his warranty. I was one step ahead of him. The Koppers representative had already done his inspection, and the warranty would be in the mail that day.

Ernie got the warranty and paid in full. I paid all the suppliers. This job put Murton Roofing of Miami back in good shape. It was a pleasure working with Ernie.

CHAPTER 6

South Carolina Ports Authority, Building 318

This building's roof was heavily damaged; half of it was missing. It also had a metal deck missing. The roof that was still there contained asbestos. There were big units blown off. This building stored big rolls of paper. At the preroof meeting, five contractors showed up. We were told that a ship was scheduled to come in with a load of paper, and the roof had to be dried in within six weeks.

The bid opening would be in one week. That did not give us very much time to get our bid together. John Bodine would get on the units that had to be replaced. The metal deck was priced in Atlanta. One of the big hurdles was getting licensed in South Carolina to remove asbestos. Murton Roofing was already licensed in Florida. I got Randy's crew in school to get licensed for asbestos removal in South Carolina. We lucked out, and there was a class that week. We had to get licensed even if we lost the bid.

When bid day came, they only got three bids. Murton Roofing of South Carolina was the lowest bidder. The second bidder, who lost by a couple thousand dollars, filed a written protest stating that Murton Roofing of South Carolina was not licensed in South Carolina to remove asbestos. We had just gotten our license that day. We produced our license, and the protest was denied. At the preconstruction meeting, we were reminded of the schedule of the ship coming in with the load of paper. We were told that there would be full-time inspections for the duration of the job.

The first thing I had to do was build a scaffold stairway to get up on the roof. The new metal for the deck would be delivered in ten days. Jerry Doxie would be the foreman on this job. He had to get all the decks squared off. Randy was going to handle all of the tear off. We also had to set up a shower for the asbestos removal. John said the units would be delivered in three weeks, and they had to be wired. I had to set up a crane with a local contractor.

We were about two weeks into the job when I got a call at five thirty in the morning to tell me that my warehouse was on fire. When I got down there, there were two fire trucks there, and all the materials inside were on fire. I had a man staying in the warehouse. His name was Hector. He had come up from Miami. He told me that two Black men had broken in and were pouring gasoline. He yelled at them and said he was inside. They yelled at him and said, "Burn, Mexican!" Hector was Cuban. He said when he got out of the warehouse, he saw them getting away in a white pickup truck. When the police got there, they made a report. I ordered two dumpsters and started cleaning out all the materials from the warehouse.

The roof had a big hole in it. It was a wooden deck. I sent one of my men to go get some lumber. By the end of the day, we had the hole fixed and had a temporary roof on. The fire did not stop us. We were up and running by the end of the day. I ordered all-new materials. I had a pretty good idea who the two guys were, but I had no proof. I did not have time to go after them. This could have been a lot worse. Hector was OK, and it just cost me a new truckload of material and some lumber.

Back at Building 318, the new metal showed up. I worked up on the roof with Jerry, and in five days, we had all the metal decking complete. Randy and his crew were tearing off every day. Once I got all the asbestos off, the job was smooth sailing from there. Jerry was putting new roof on every day; he was getting along with the inspector. The new units showed up in four weeks, and John had all the wiring done. We set the units in place with the crane.

The job was almost complete when Charlie asked me to look at the headquarters building. He said he did not need to go out for bids on the repairs. All the metal was ripped off, and the leader heads and downspouts were gone. I had Dave look at it with me and give me a price. It had some roof work that had to be done.

I gave Charlie the price, and he gave me the go-ahead. They were slow on getting my payment on Building 318, but once they got their money, they paid up.

The boat showed up in five weeks. Jerry was all dry-in. He had another week of detail work before it was complete. This was a successful job, and the final contract was $648,000. Dave got started on the headquarters building; it was all copper work, and he did a nice job. The roof work was minor. We finished the headquarters building and got paid promptly. Working with the South Charleston Ports Authority was demanding, and Murton Roofing of South Carolina met all of their demands.

CHAPTER 7

Rainbow Market—Mary Wilson

Stanley asked if I could help out a close friend of his. Her name was Mary Wilson, and she was the owner of the Rainbow Market. She lived on East Bay Street. Stanley said she was an older woman and very tough. He made the appointment.

I went to meet her. She lived in a three-story house; it was a mansion. When we met, she was concerned I was from Miami. She said the Rainbow Market had severe damage to the roof. She gave me the address. It was 40 North Market Street. I told her I would look at it. The next day, I went to look at it and saw she was right: it had severe damage. Most of the deck was blown off. The brick walls were blown out. I had to call Nelson and David to meet me out there.

When Nelson saw it, he said it was a major repair. All the bricks would have to be put back. He said that he and David could do it. He said they would need a drawing and a permit to do the work on the deck.

When I met with Mary and told her I would need a drawing and a permit, she told me not to worry about the permit. She needed the price to fix the deck and for a new roof. I worked out the price. It came to $98,000 with 30 percent down. When she looked at the price, she said it was double what it should be. She told me she had been in construction for thirty years and that she would need a day or two to think it over.

On the third day, Mary called me and asked me to come over. When I got there, she was ready. She offered $90,000 with a 10 percent deposit with draws on work completed. She had the check ready for $9,000, and I made the deal.

When I told Nelson, he said it would take four days to clean all the debris out. Then he and David could start work on replacing all the brick. Mary told me the construction was done in 1978.

Nelson said the building was at least fifty to sixty years old. He gave me a list of what he needed for the deck. It consisted of beams and wood decking. When they started cleaning up all the debris, the tenants below started to move back in. I told them no way; they were not in the dry. When Nelson had all the beams in, an inspector showed up on the job. He asked Nelson for the permit. He shut the job down.

When I told Mary, she said she would take care of it. I don't know what she did, but within two days, she had the drawing and the permit. Nelson went back to work. The tenants moving in under us was too dangerous, so we had to switch up and start working at night. When all the roof deck was finished, the next draw was ready. It was for $35,000.

Mary came to the job to inspect the work; she was satisfied with the work and paid the $35,000 draw. She told me at that time she would not pay any more until the job was complete. That was not the agreement, but I did not have any choice in the matter.

Jerry Doxie and his crew did all the roofing work in three days. The building was 100 percent in the dry. There was some sheet metal work to do. Dave and his crew got all the metal work complete. When I went to Mary with the final bill, she said she wanted to wait for two heavy rains to check for leaks. It was about two weeks when two rains came, and there were no leaks. When I went to meet Mary, the final bill was $46,000. She gave me a check for $36,000 with writing on it that said "paid in full for work on Rainbow Market."

She said I made out good on that job, and if I had a problem, I could take her to court and not cash the check. I went straight to Stanley; he was an attorney, and I needed some advice. He said he was surprised that she would do that, but Mary knew every judge in town, and I would not have any chance. He said, "Cash the check." I did.

Rainbow Market

CHAPTER 8

C. E. Williams School

This was one of the last schools to be reroofed. It was the band room. We had to do a moisture test to the deck. It was lightweight concrete. The test came back that the lightweight concrete was soaking wet. The whole deck had to be removed. This was a two-story building separate from the school; it was a dangerous job.

Thanksgiving weekend was coming up. It was perfect timing; no kids were in school. We had to get two dumpsters in. Everything was set up; we were going to have two crews in, Terry's crew and Jerry's crew. When I told my wife we had to work, she was upset. This was our first holiday in our house on Folly Beach. She said, "You have been working seven days a week for a year."

When Friday came around, everybody showed up. We started the tear off, and everything was going well. I was working with the crew up on the roof. We were setting the new metal deck, and I told the other man on the deck we needed another inch. Instead, he moved it six inches and knocked my foot off the beam. I went through the roof, and my arm got caught on the beam. My weight pulled me down off the beam, and I fell two stories down. When I landed, there was a music stand that went into my leg. The fall pulled my arm out of the socket. My bone was sticking out by my neck. I had to go to the hospital.

My son was working on the job. I told Terry and Jerry to keep working and had my son take me to the hospital. When we got there, the doctor looked at it and said it was completely out of the socket. He said he would have to operate unless they could get it back in the socket. There were two ambulance drivers there and my son. He gave me something for pain, and the two men and my son grabbed my arm and started to pull. Somehow, they got it back into the socket. It hurt bad. The doctor was looking at the X-rays and told me the rotor cuff was completely torn. He said if it didn't heal, they would have to operate. He gave me a sling and some pain pills and released me.

It was getting dark outside, and I told my son to take me back to the job. When we got there, both crews were on the ground. They said all the new deck was on, and they would put the roof on Saturday. I had my son drive me home.

When we got there, my wife asked what happened. I told her I had had a minor accident. My leg hurt worse than my arm did. That musical stand that went into my leg left a big hole in the back of it. I told my son to pick me up in the morning. When he did, my wife was not talking to me.

When we got to the school, all the crews were there. Jerry, who was on the other end of the metal deck, said he was sorry. I told him, "That was yesterday. Let's get this roof on." We worked all day and completed the roof. We had to come back on Sunday to finish some detail work.

My leg was killing me. There was a bruise bigger than a softball there. I told my son Ed to pick me up in the morning, and he said, "Dad, we got it tomorrow. We will be done in a half a day."

I said, "Pick me up. I want to see this done 100 percent."

My son picked me up, and we finished in a half a day. Monday morning, I told Sharon to bill Ray and to hand-deliver it to him. I could not put my belt on for about a year. My rotator cuff somehow healed itself, and I did not need an operation. The hole in my leg still bothers me when it is cold. The scar is still there. It reminds me of C. E. Williams thirty years later.

CHAPTER 9

Charleston Naval Base—Building 198, Headquarters Building

The base was closed to all civilian traffic. About a year after the storm, it was open. The first building they wanted to get reroofed was the headquarters building. They invited four roofing contractors to the prebid. They hired a consultant from the navy. He said they would be very specific on the details, and in the specification, there would be no changes. When we visited the roof, some of the details would not work. When we questioned them, we were told again there would be no changes. Murton Roofing's bid was about $550,000. It was low. States Roofing from Alabama was the second bid.

At the preconstruction meeting, the consultant was again reminding us there would be no changes.

We were having a hard time getting a setup for our equipment when we finally agreed the setup was on the far end of the building. We started on the hardest areas on the roof. There were air-conditioning and large units on this area. On our third day of tear off, they were cleaning around a leg on the air-conditioning when a brick fell through the ceiling. It crashed into a glass enclosure that housed a Polaris submarine—the first submarine that was built on the base in 1955. When the brick went through the glass, it landed on the nose of the submarine and took a big chunk out of it.

When the colonel saw it, he flipped out. He said that it was dedicated in 1956 and could not be replaced. I told him I would get it fixed. He told me it better be perfect. It was a joke around the office: the roofing contractor sank the Polaris submarine. It was not a joke when I went to get it fixed. The company that built it was no longer in business. I had to find someone who could fix this. The colonel would not let it leave the premises; I found a guy who did nothing but repair statues. He came to look at it. He told me it would be $6,500 to do it on the premises. I agreed to it, and he started work on it. Now I had to get someone to build a glass aquarium to house the submarine. I found a guy who could do it; his price was $2,100. When it was completed, the colonel was happy.

It was the day after Christmas. Terry wanted to work. I was at home; it was a foggy day. I was watching the Weather Channel. It did not show any rain at eight o'clock. I told him to cut it but only take a little piece. He cut it and removed the roof. Around ten, Terry called me and said it was raining. He was trying to cover the roof with tarps. I got dressed and headed to the job. When I got there and went inside, the lay-in ceilings were all down. There were about twenty desks that this ceiling had landed on. It was a big mess.

There was a maintenance man there. He was the only person in the building. All the rest were gone on Christmas vacation. I told him if he helped me clean up the mess, I would pay him. He agreed. He went and got a pallet of rags, and we started spreading them around. He brought empty trash barrels. By about one o'clock, the rain had passed. Terry got the roof dried in. The crew and I worked until nine o'clock that night, and we got everything cleaned up. All we had to do was get the ceiling tiles back in.

The maintenance man did not have enough ceiling tiles to do the ceiling. He gave me the number of the ceiling tiles. I called around and found them. I went and got twelve cartons of ceiling tile. The next day, we got all the ceiling done. It looked like no one had ever been in there. I gave the maintenance man $2,500 for saving me and helping me clean up. We took the rest of the week off and got started after the first. I have never worked between Christmas and New Year's since that day.

The rest of the job went pretty smoothly. The consultant changed some of his details, and we had a good relationship with him. He was going to be on every job. They had over $5 million in reroofing work.

CHAPTER 10

Charleston Naval Base—Building 41

We had the same consultant that we had had for Building 198. At the preconference meeting, it was expressed to us this was an asbestos removal, and we had to take all precautions. This building was also a high-security building. We would have to fill out special forms and get a high-security badge. Our bid came in low, and we were awarded the contract.

When we went to the preconstruction meeting, we received the special forms to fill out. There were eight men in the crew; only two passed for the badge. Even Terry failed; this was a problem. We had to have a meeting with the top man. He said the only way he would approve them was if we had a person assigned to us full time. We would also have to pay him. I agreed.

When we went to start work, they told us all the equipment would have to be removed daily and then checked in every day. This was because of the Polaris equipment stored inside. All the asbestos would have to be bagged and identified on a red label. We were used to just double lining the dumpster. We never bagged the tear off and labeled it. Back in 1991, asbestos removal was fairly new. The naval base was a target because at one time asbestos was mandatory on all ships.

Now I knew why we were the low bidder. This was a very difficult job; plus, there were all the rules we had to follow. We were getting through the job. There was a big tile job coming up; it was in the housing section. There were eight or ten houses that needed to be reroofed. It was a million-dollar job. At the prebid, we had the same consultant. The houses were one story with easy access. I had one of the best tile crews in Miami. When I bid it, the bid was tight. I really wanted this job. At the bid opening, I was just below $1 million. States Roofing of Alabama was at $800,000. He was $200,000 below me. I waited for about two weeks, thinking he would withdraw his bid. I went in to talk to the roof consultant to see what was going on. He told me States Roofing of Alabama had already signed the contract and was working on the job. I could not believe it; I went straight over to the job.

There were thirty men on the job, and they were working on four houses. There was a gentleman standing by a red Corvette. I went over to him and introduced myself. He told me he was the owner, Roy Gillespie. Roy and I became friends. Roy came to Miami during Hurricane Andrew and worked with Murton Roofing of Miami.

CHAPTER 11

Gordon H. Garrett Academy
of Technology

In June of 1993, Sharon got a call from a woman who said she got our phone number from Owen Cornings. The woman worked for an insurance company. I called her and made an appointment to meet her at the high school the next day. She was from North Carolina; she was a big woman, and she meant business.

Pelham had just filed bankruptcy, and this new addition was ready for roofing. The general contractor was nervous. Pelham had had most of the material delivered to the job. It was uncovered and exposed to the weather. Pelham had been paid $50,000 for it, but none of it was installed. All the material was in the weather and could not be used. She said she had

$181,000, minus the $50,000 for materials, to do the job. I told her I would get back with her after I figured out the price. She said, "No, I want to award it today."

She said we could go into the contractor's trailer and get measurements; she also told me she had two other bonded jobs that Pelham had abandoned. They were big. When we got in the trailer, the superintendent from the job was furious and upset that Pelham had done him that way with the material. He said he wanted men on the job the next day. I told her I would work with the $181,000 minus the material that could be used. She told me the names of the other two jobs: Turbeville Correctional Institution and Ridgeland Correctional Institution. I said, "Let's go to Turbeville now."

We drove to Turbeville. Pelham had three buildings mopped in. The next day, we met at Ridgeland. It was a little behind Turbeville. The first building was just getting ready for a roof. It was at this meeting she told me she was going to talk to Fort Roofing out of Sumter. She said Owen Cornings gave her that number. I made a deal on all three jobs. She said she could have all the paperwork done in one day. I told her as soon as I had all the paperwork, I would start Garrett's addition. She got the paperwork the next day, and Jerry and his crew started work that day. They had to separate all the material and order new material. The job went pretty smoothly from there on out. It was a fact now that Murton Roofing of South Carolina was the largest roofing contractor in Charleston, South Carolina.

CHAPTER 12

Turbeville Correctional Institution

When I went to a meeting with the superintendent of the job, he was surprised that Pelham Roofing had filed for bankruptcy. He said he had known Pelham Roofing for twenty years; he couldn't believe that Roger Parker would not give him any notice of the filing. The superintendent said he was happy with the crew that was working, and he would set up a meeting with me and the foreman from Pelham.

When I met with the foreman (I'm not going to mention his name), I asked him if he had set my warehouse on fire two years earlier. I said that I had hired some men from Pelham, and they said he was bragging that he had set the fire. He denied it and said that was just a rumor. If he would have admitted it, I probably would have hired him. I just could not hire him. The superintendent was upset; he really wanted me to hire him.

They were on the third building out of ten, and none of the details were done. When I looked at the details submitted and approved, I saw there were none. Pelham did not submit any. With no details submitted, we had to submit new drawings. We had to get all Pelham equipment off the job and get our own equipment in the first two weeks. It was tough. Randy and the superintendent were not getting along. After two weeks, they started to get along.

By this time, Randy and his crew were on the fifth building. All the details submitted were approved. When the manufacturer's representative did his inspections, everything passed. He was pleased with the quality of work. This was a fast-track job. When Randy got done with the tenth building, it was about five weeks. The manufacturer's representative issued the warranty, and the general contractor was happy that everything had worked out. The bonding company was happy. Both Garrett Academy and Turbeville were complete. Now we just had Ridgeland to complete.

Turbeville Correctional Facility

CHAPTER 13

Ridgeland Correctional Institution

This contract was for eleven buildings. Pelham had done nothing on this job except sign the contract and give them a payment and performance bond. We had to do all the submittals and apply for the warranty. All the submittals were approved. Jerry was the foreman on this job. It was like Turbeville, fast track.

The superintendent and Jerry were getting along great. When Jerry was on the fifth building, the manufacturer's representative did his inspection, and he was good to go with the quality of the workmanship. He said he would be back for the final.

The contract amount Pelham agreed to was good enough to do the job. The general contractor had to pay the bonding company; in the end, the bonding company didn't have to take any money out of pocket. She was happy about that. Out of the three jobs, the only money the bonding company spent was for the material at the Garrett Academy and the money Pelham received at Turbeville for work completed.

Jerry was on the job for about six weeks when he completed it. The manufacturer's representative did his final inspection and issued the warranty. This was in late 1994. Work was getting hard to come by in Charleston. I made a decision to move to Columbia, South Carolina. There was plenty of bonded work bidding in Columbia.

Ridgeland Correctional Institute